WIDE OPEN SPACES

Text and Paintings by

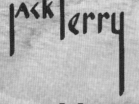

HARVEST HOUSE PUBLISHERS

EUGENE, OREGON

Wide Open Spaces

Text copyright © 2004 by Jack Terry
Published by Harvest House Publishers
Eugene, Oregon 97402
www.harvesthousepublishers.com

Library of Congress Cataloging-in-Publication Data

Terry, Jack, 1952-
   Wide open spaces / text and painting by Jack Terry.
      p. cm.
   ISBN 0-7369-1310-6
  1. Nature—Religious aspects—Christianity. 2. Outdoor life—Alaska.
I. Title.
   BT695.5.T467 2004
   242—dc22

                        2004001054

Artwork designs are reproduced under license from © Arts Uniq' ®, Inc., Cookeville, TN and
may not be reproduced without permission. For more information regarding art prints featured
in this book, please contact:
   Jack Terry Fine Art, Ltd.
   4925 Bandera Hwy.
   Kerrville, TX 78028
   (830) 634-2053
   www.jackterryart.com

Design & production by Koechel Peterson & Associates, Minneapolis, MN

Harvest House Publishers has made every effort to trace the ownership of all poems and quotes.
In the event of a question arising from the use of a poem or quote, we regret any error made
and will be pleased to make the necessary correction in future editions of this book.

Scripture quotations are taken from the Holy Bible, New International Version®, Copyright©
1973, 1978, 1984 by the International Bible Society. Used by permission of Zondervan
Publishing House.

Printed in Hong Kong

04 05 06 07 08 09 10 11 12 / NG / 10 9 8 7 6 5 4 3 2 1

DEDICATION

To the furthering of the kingdom of our Creator

SPECIAL THANKS

J.W. and Dawn Smith for the ultimate Alaskan adventure

My friend and brother Ray Durham for his godly wisdom

Harvest House Publishers for the opportunity to share my experience

Rusty Pool for the friendship of a lifetime

Marc Bennett for his professional photography

CONTENTS

As evening falls and while I seek thy face in prayer,

grant unto me the joy of good friends…

and the peace of the quiet heart.

PERCY ROY HOWARD

GROWING UP
— IN THE —
GREAT OUTDOORS

MOST FOLKS FIND NATURE and the great outdoors fascinating. My fascination with them began in early childhood. The simplicity of whiling away the time skipping rocks across a shallow pond with some pals or climbing trees and playing king of the jungle brought so much pleasure. Some of my fondest memories are of spending hot summer days trampling over dusty, crimson rocks and sand, dodging the thorny mesquite limbs by keeping a step behind my grandmother on the way to one of her "sure enough" good catfish holes in rural west Texas.

My uncle Billy Bob always tagged along toting our poles, certain to get the fishing line tangled into a web of unusable proportions while muttering muffled frustrations under his breath. He often tripped over the dangling mess he had created and would find himself entangled in a dusty pile of debris amongst the rocks and cactus. Oh, the joys of fishing. What a time we had together!

When we finally arrived at the fishing hole and got our bait in the water, we would just sit back on the bank and enjoy the day. Red-tailed hawks and buzzards circled in the sky above us while jackrabbits with long, erect ears stood like statues in the shade of the prickly pear cacti. The now almost-extinct horned toads, looking like miniature dinosaurs, crawled tirelessly across the cracked red ground in search of ants and other insects to devour. Grandmother reminisced about the old times. Just when I was completely enthralled in one of her stories, a bobber would sink and the water would splash with the sound of a big one on the line. By the end of the day, we'd have a stringer full of catfish—almost as big as the smile on my face.

After fishing, Grandmother always let me drive her Buick sedan down the rural dirt roads before we reached the blacktop leading to her house. Once home, we enjoyed fried catfish as the sweet reward for a good day's work. When the stars began to sparkle, it was off for a bath and just one more story before our perfect day came to a close. My fond dreams of the big one that didn't get away were only interrupted by the sunlight of a new day filled with even greater expectations.

My grandmother loved to go fishing because she understood life's simple pleasures. She saw the beauty of the great outdoors as a gift from God that is to be shared and enjoyed, and she savored every moment. I am very thankful she passed that great heritage down to me.

Through the years, I have been privileged to hunt for elk in the wilderness of the Rocky Mountains, ducks in the swamps of east Texas, and trophy deer in the thick brush of south Texas. I have fished for bull reds in the Gulf of Mexico and northern pike in the frigid waters of Canada. I have hiked to the peaks of majestic waterfalls in Yosemite National Park and flown between the towering rock walls of the Grand Canyon.

I have watched the leaves change colors right before my very eyes in the rolling hills of Maine.

A recent trip to New England encouraged me to ponder some aspects about the great outdoors from a different perspective. I discovered I have been taking the freedom of nature for granted.

While I have immensely enjoyed my many adventures, I had lost sight of what a privilege it is to have the opportunity to truly enjoy such things. I was reminded of the history of our great nation and the sacrifice the early settlers made so we might enjoy our various freedoms. For several evenings, I sat watching the sunset on the harbor of the quaint fishing village of Camden, Maine. I thought about the masted schooners docked below and how the early pilgrims spent many perilous months at sea as they pursued American soil. The freedom we have today to experience all this wonderful country came at a high cost. We are indeed a blessed nation in many ways.

It is with much gratitude to God, our founding fathers, my family, and my teachers that I would like to share some of my observations and experiences in the great outdoors. For six amazing days in the Alaskan wilderness, I was totally overwhelmed by the handiwork of God's creation. While mere words and pigments brushed upon a canvas cannot accurately express my feelings, I urge you to draw from your own personal experiences. Bask for a few moments in the wonderful world of the great outdoors. It is a very special gift from God, preserved by our forefathers to be shared and enjoyed by each of us and all generations to come.

Climb the mountains and get their good tidings.
Nature's peace will flow into you as sunshine flows into trees.
The winds will blow their own freshness into you, and the storms their energy,
while cares will drop off like autumn leaves.

JOHN MUIR

IN THE BEGINNING...

HOW OFTEN WE TAKE the world around us for granted. As the pressures and deadlines of our society continually pull us in all directions, it can be difficult to enjoy life's beautiful surroundings. If we would only slow down and open our eyes, we would find a glorious world has been created for us to enjoy.

God created the magnificent planet earth where we are blessed to live. This earth supplies all our physical needs plus great beauty and pleasure. When we stand in awe of snow-covered peaks, roaring waterfalls, crystal-clear streams and turquoise-blue oceans, and satellite images of our universe, we are merely observing only a portion of the beauty and holiness of God Himself.

David wrote these beautiful words in Psalm 8: "O LORD, our Lord, how majestic is your name in all the earth! You have set your glory above the heavens . . . When I consider your heavens, the work of your fingers, the moon and the stars, which you have set in place, what is man that you are mindful of him, the son of man that you care for him? You made him a little lower than the heavenly beings and crowned him with glory and honor. You make him ruler over the works of your hands; you put everything under his feet; all flocks and herds, and the beasts of the field, the birds of the air, and the fish of the sea, all that swim the paths of the seas. O LORD, our Lord, how majestic is your name in all the earth!"

Perhaps that is the reason man has from the beginning of time dared to climb the highest mountains, explore outer space, and venture to the bottom of the world's oceans. Whether you enjoy rock climbing, scuba diving, hunting, fishing, horseback riding, cycling, bird-watching, golf, or just an afternoon picnic in a field clothed in wild flowers, the glory of God is all around you.

Genesis 1:1 says, "In the beginning God created the heavens and the earth." Contained in this simple verse are more facts than my limited mind can comprehend. Modern science can tell us many things about our universe that causes me to simply stand in overwhelming awe of God's power and creativity. The galaxy we live in is spinning at the speed of 490,000 miles per hour but still needs 200 million years to complete one rotation. Astronomers estimate our galaxy contains more than 30 billion suns, many of which are larger than our sun, which is more than 1.5 million times larger than earth. Our galaxy, the Milky Way, is thought to be 200,000 light years in diameter, with light traveling at 186,000 miles per second. Modern science believes there is considerably more beyond it.

Words cannot accurately describe how truly incredible God is, much less the infinite beauty of our universe. It's hard for me to comprehend that some believe our world came into existence almost accidentally. The glorious palette filled with infinite colors that paint our earthly home and the heavens above is the masterpiece from God's brush. The apostle Paul wrote in Romans 1:20, "For since the creation of the world God's invisible qualities—his eternal power and divine nature—have been clearly seen, being understood from what has been made, so that men are without excuse." If we can't see God's power and understand His nature through all He has created, perhaps it is time to put our busy schedules aside and spend a few days in the great outdoors.

Jesus enjoyed the outdoors during His years on earth. He spent time alone in the desert, on the mountains, and in the gardens. He had a particular fondness for the sea. He prayed on the sea, walked on the water, preached, and fed multitudes from the sea.

He also had a heart for fishermen. One day while walking by the Sea of Galilee, He chose a group of fishermen to be His followers. These outdoorsmen understood the concept of casting nets and fishing. Jesus said to them "Come, and I will make you fishers of men."

Jesus understood the concept of fishing and realized the physical event of enjoying good company, beautiful surroundings, and good food here on earth was a reflection of the larger spiritual event to come. As He fellowshipped with His friends in the great outdoors here on earth, He invited all of mankind to fellowship with Him in the glorious surroundings of His heavenly home and to eat food from His heavenly table. His invitation still stands today.

PSALM 104

Praise the LORD, O my soul.

O LORD my God, you are very great; you are clothed with splendor and majesty. He wraps himself in light as with a garment; he stretches out the heavens like a tent and lays the beams of his upper chambers on their waters. He makes the clouds his chariot and rides on the wings of the wind.

He set the earth on its foundations; it can never be moved. You covered it with the deep as with a garment; the waters stood above the mountains. But at your rebuke the waters fled, at the sound of your thunder they took to flight; they flowed over the mountains, they went down into the valleys, to the place you assigned for them. You set a boundary they cannot cross; never again will they cover the earth.

He makes springs pour water into the ravines; it flows between the mountains. They give water to all the beasts of the fields; the wild donkeys quench their thirst. The birds of the air nest by the waters; they sing among the branches. He waters the mountains from his upper chambers; the earth is satisfied by the fruit of his work.

He makes grass grow for the cattle, and plants for man to cultivate— bringing forth food from the earth: wine that gladdens the heart of man, oil to make his face shine, and bread that sustains his heart. The trees of the LORD are well watered, the cedars of Lebanon that he planted. There the birds make their nests; the stork has its home in the pine trees. The high mountains belong to the wild goats; the crags are a refuge for the coneys.

The moon marks off the seasons, and the sun knows when to go down. You bring darkness, it becomes night, and all the beasts of the forest prowl. The lions roar for their prey and seek their food from God. The sun rises, and they steal away; they return and lie down in their dens. Then man goes out to his work, to his labor until evening.

How many are your works, O LORD! In wisdom you made them all; the earth is full of your creatures. There is the sea, vast and spacious, teeming with creatures beyond number—living things both large and small. There the ships go to and fro, and the leviathan, which you formed to frolic there.

These all look to you to give them their food at the proper time. When you give it to them, they gather it up; when you open your hand, they are satisfied with good things. When you hide your face, they are terrified; when you take away their breath, they die and return to the dust. When you send your Spirit, they are created, and you renew the face of the earth.

May the glory of the LORD endure forever; may the LORD rejoice in his works—he who looks at the earth, and it trembles, who touches the mountains, and they smoke. I will sing to the LORD all my life; I will sing praise to my God as long as I live. May my meditation be pleasing to him, as I rejoice in the LORD. But may sinners vanish from the earth and the wicked be no more.

Praise the LORD, O my soul. Praise the LORD.

To go fishing is the chance to wash one's soul
with pure air, with the rush of the brook,
or with the shimmer of sun on blue water.

HERBERT HOOVER

THE LAST
~ GREAT ~
FRONTIER

THOUGH I HAVE SPENT a great deal of time outdoors and visited many secluded places, I have never experienced the magnitude and glory of creation as in the Alaskan wilderness. Being from Texas, I understand the term "big," but Alaska is truly a territory like no other. It is a beautiful, rugged, and wild land of incredible towering mountains, slow-moving glaciers, active volcanoes, broad valleys, pristine lakes and rivers, hot springs and icy streams, rocky coastlines, waterfalls, dense coniferous forests, and an abundance of fish, birds and wildlife.

In the summer of my 50th year, I was invited to spend a week fly-fishing for migrating salmon with my life-long friend and outdoorsman, Rusty Pool, in the wilderness on the Alaskan Peninsula. I knew very little about Alaska outside of Eskimos, igloos, and oil wells, but I jumped at the opportunity to see an area so few people have set foot on before.

The word Alaska is derived from an Aleut word meaning "great land." It is known as the Last Frontier because of its opportunities and sparse population. The 2002 population census was around 627,000 for the entire state that has a total area of 615,230 square miles. Alaska has more total area of lakes and rivers than any other state, equaling more than the entire land area of Massachusetts and Vermont combined. There are more than 100,000 glaciers in Alaska, some larger than the state of Rhode Island.

My first glimpse of the magnitude of the 49th state was from my small airplane window some 30,000 feet above the grandiose landscape. All I could see for hours en route to King Salmon were the snow-covered mountains of the Alaska Range and Brooks Range. They seemed to travel endlessly in both directions as far as the eye could see. I was absolutely mesmerized by the expanse of the mountains and the size of the crystal blue glaciers frigidly nestled between the icy slopes. As the flight progressed, I could see Mt. McKinley on the horizon far to the north. It rises 20,320 feet above sea level, almost four miles high, and towers like a giant over the surrounding mountains. Seventeen of the 20 largest mountains in the United States are in Alaska. My excitement was building with the passing of each mile. I was beginning to grasp the enormity of the wilderness below.

Much of Alaska is inaccessible by roads due to the arduous landscape, so the next phase of our journey would be a two-and-a-half-hour flight from King Salmon to our camp on the Alaska Peninsula in a tiny four-passenger plane. At the helm of our rather ragged blue and rusty Cessna, was a former military pilot who, like many others, had chosen to make a life for himself flying people into the bush where few would dare to venture.

The Alaska Peninsula is a rugged land filled with impressive beauty. It includes nearly 16 million acres, which is relatively small in comparison to the mainland. The mountains of the Aleutian Range comprise the backbone of the peninsula. The peninsula is composed of towering mountains, broad valleys, foggy fjords, and often steep and rocky coastlines. Glacial lakes, rich tundra, and 14 major volcanoes, including 9 that are still active, are scattered throughout the region. It is a habitat for 222 species of resident and migratory wildlife. The Becharof National Wildlife Refuge has calculated there are 30 species of terrestrial mammals, 11 species of marine mammals, 146 bird species, and 35 species of fish. Sea lions, otters, seals, seabirds, and waterfowl inhabit the coastal areas. Bald eagles, hawks, falcons, and owls nest on the rock pinnacles and spires along the coast. The tundra lowlands are host to caribou, moose, brown bear, wolves, swans, and other waterfowl. What an amazing place it is!

Brown or "grizzly" bears make use of all the land

from the mountaintops to the coastline. They roam the tundra in search of roots, berries, ground squirrels, and other small burrowing animals when their preferred diet of salmon are unavailable.

Thousands of caribou migrate along the peninsula each year as their ancestors have for centuries. Unlike most species of deer, these animals spend their entire lives on the move.

To observe the Alaska Peninsula is like stepping back in time hundreds, even thousands, of years and viewing the earth as it was originally created—unspoiled by the hands of man, raw and natural—just as God had designed it.

God saw all that he had made,

and it was very good.

THE BOOK OF GENESIS

⟡ HOME FOR A WEEK ⟡

OUR FLIGHT INTO CAMP was a magnificent sight. We soared over hundreds of miles of winding rivers, lush green valleys, herds of caribou, dozens of large, brown grizzly bears, bald eagles, and even the mouth of a steaming volcano.

As we began our descent on the south side of the volcano, I got my first glimpse of the Pacific Ocean on the southern horizon and knew we were approaching our final destination. Nakalilok Bay occupied the inlet between the ocean and the volcano and was surrounded by a horseshoe of lush green mountains and rolling hills. They were covered with tall pink flowers known as fireweed and rather short, dense alder trees creating a heavy cover of brush, a perfect habitat for bears. Rivers and streams crookedly flowed into the bay from the snowcapped peaks. I saw the tents of our camp perched on a steep hill along the shoreline overlooking the bay. As I peered down below us into the water, it suddenly occurred to me there was no place to land the plane! The hills were too steep and the narrow shoreline was covered with rocks and outcroppings.

Upon my rather loud inquisition, the seasoned pilot said "Not to worry, I'll put her down right there." He pointed out the tiny window to a narrow stretch of beach along the base of a hill just north of camp and adjacent to the bay. I later found out that a plane is only able to land there when the tidewaters are out, and in the absence of thick fog that frequently seeps into the bay from the Pacific Ocean. The tides seem to be rather unpredictable on the peninsula and no one is able to accurately pinpoint their exact schedule. In the wilderness, there are no weather or radio stations so much depends upon the instincts and expertise of the

pilot. Our landing went smoothly and our guides for the week-long adventure soon greeted us. As we stepped off the plane, we immediately saw bear tracks in the wet sand. Upon a closer look, they were everywhere and they were big. Leaving their imprints in long winding paths from the beach, they disappeared into the grassy hills beyond or around the craggy coastline. At that moment, I knew my dream of a true wilderness adventure had just begun.

I absolutely could not believe the amount of cargo we unloaded from that small plane. It would have been a tight fit to cram it all in a Greyhound bus. The fact we even got off the ground was a miracle. After several trips up the steep hand-hewn trail to camp with our gear and rations, we were ready to catch our breath and take in the sights around us.

The sky was baby blue with a few white billowy clouds and the air was so fresh I was certain no man or beast had ever breathed it before. To the north was the towering 8,400-foot high volcano we had just flown over. It was eight miles away, but because of its enormity it seemed much closer. To the south was the immense marine-blue Pacific Ocean disappearing into eternity. A chain of islands was visible along the horizon—the largest is Kodiak Island, home of the biggest grizzly bears on earth. We watched mammoth whales as they swam and spewed in the icy waters between our camp and the islands. Across the bay to the east was a mountain range where a volcano had erupted ages ago leaving a rusty-ore and golden sulfur-stained caldron silhouetted against the brilliant white snowcaps. Suddenly from around the rocky shoreline below flew a bald eagle, landing on the beach just below us. I could hardly believe my eyes. His brilliant white head of feathers glowed in the sun like a kingly crown.

He sat majestically near the water and enjoyed the warmth of the sun's rays. He was the first of many eagles we would see in their native habitat.

Our camp was a sight to behold. It belongs to my friends J.W. and Dawn Smith who have guided fishermen in Alaska for many years during a few weeks every summer while the weather is tolerable and the quality of fishing is unsurpassed. They lease the land from the state and have a wonderful facility. All the supplies are stored in a bear-proof cache built of logs that have drifted up on the shoreline over the years. There are no trees large enough in the area to provide such a shelter. Every log was hand-carried from the distant Pacific coastline where they wash up from far away places. Fresh water was tapped-in from a spring on the hillside just above us for cooking, drinking, and bathing. Small propane bottles were flown in to service the cook stoves in the kitchen tent and hot showers. Thankfully, there were no telephones or electricity, but I must admit the hot water and delicious home-cooked meals made the Alaska wilderness even more heavenly.

That afternoon, after everyone was settled in, the lure of the salmon began to call. We trekked down the hill decked in waders, vests, and raincoats, with rods in hand, ready to sample some of that notoriously good fishing. The temperatures in mid-July are mild but it can get very windy, sometimes blowing up to 40 and 50 miles per hour which makes controlling a fly rod somewhat challenging. Occasional light to very heavy rain can occur almost any time of day and the waters in the bay, rivers, and streams are very cold as a result of melting snow and glaciers. Proper gear is a necessity. Along with all of the standard equipment, I packed two or more cameras at all times. I found myself carrying quite a load. That afternoon we would stay in the immediate area below camp, but on subsequent days Rusty and I became more adventuresome, hiking several miles a day. I wanted to leave no stone of this wilderness adventure unturned.

As we followed the bear tracks along the shoreline toward our fishing spot, I noticed the tide was beginning to enter the bay and fill the lowest areas of the riverbed. It was shortly thereafter that the salmon began to make their way from the ocean, into the shallow waters of the bay. They were swimming upstream to the rivers at the base of the northern hills to spawn. It wasn't long before the bay was full of water and migrating salmon. It was time to fish!

We were hoping to catch any of the five varieties of Pacific salmon that afternoon: reds (sockeye), pinks, kings (chinook), chums, or silvers (coho), and maybe some Dolly Varden trout. It wasn't long before "Got him," and "There he is," echoed from the rising waters. What a fight they put up, especially on fly rods. Tips bent toward the water like candlesticks in the hot sun. It took anywhere from 10 to 20 minutes to land a fish, especially the big chums and kings. What a great couple of hours it was! We caught fish with almost every single cast.

All of the fish we caught that week were released so they could continue their swim upstream to complete their life cycle, with the exception of a few for some very special meals. The life cycle of the salmon is a miracle of creation, a truly fascinating story we will discuss later on.

After fishing we trudged through the water to a large rock outcropping near the shoreline for a better vantage point. As we were observing the salmon below the surface, we heard a strange noise behind us coming from deep within the fallen rocks. In a few moments, a female sea otter emerged with five young ones. It appeared we were intruding on the privacy of their home about five feet from where we were sitting. They scurried off into the cold water of the bay and proceeded to swim and play as if they were putting on a show for us. The six fuzzy little creatures carried on with their routine until we went back up the hill for dinner, undaunted by our curiosity.

After a wonderfully relaxing dinner that evening, and before we retired to our tents, J.W. discussed the agenda for the next few days. The last thing on his list was "bears." He verified a fact that I had already surmised—we were camped in their backyard. Every precaution was taken not to attract the bears. All food scraps were disposed of in the bay each evening and all other trash was burned. If anyone heard or saw a bear in camp at night, we were to scream "bear" at the top of our lungs to alert everyone else. We were assured the bears were as scared of us as we were of them, and they would spook away from loud noises. But for everyone's safety, every precaution must be observed.

J.W. related a story of how a bear stuck its head inside his tent one night. He said he was so startled that he reached out and punched it in the nose and sent the bear running. Knowing J.W. the way I do, he's just fearless enough to do something like that. I preferred the alternative method which is to stand in groups of three or more, scream loudly, and wave our arms. I'd rather not chance leaving my body parts in the Alaskan wilderness as a souvenir for some big bear to brag about. As a last resort, the guides were armed with shotguns filled with pepper spray and buckshot designed specifically not to kill the bears but simply spook them away. This technique would be demonstrated more than once out of necessity before our adventure would end.

It is important to note that brown bears are huge animals. Adult females this time of year average 400 to 500 pounds. Males range from 500 to 900 pounds with some giants reaching 1,200 pounds or more. They are massive animals that can run at speeds of up to 35 or

40 miles per hour. They can catch a horse in a short distance so you can take it to the bank, you won't outrun one! Many are over nine feet tall when they stand on their hind legs. I personally watched several large bears that week stand up when they caught our scent or when they were searching for salmon in the water. They are very intimidating creatures with extremely large teeth and sharp claws.

When the "bear briefing" concluded, I headed off to my cozy sleeping bag around 9:30 p.m. for a good night's rest before our first full day of fishing. It was at least three hours before I was able to doze off, partly due to the fact it didn't get dark until almost midnight, but primarily because my eyes and ears were on high alert. I took a few minutes to make some journal entries and then just laid back and listened to the sounds of the wilderness. I heard the cries of seagulls feeding along the shoreline and an occasional wolf howl in the distance. The waves from the Pacific Ocean crashing on the rocky coastline sang me to sleep. I awoke, most thankfully, the next morning with the rising sun and all of my limbs still attached.

JUST ANOTHER DAY
— IN —
PARADISE

THE SAME BRIGHT SUN I dozed off with the night before woke me the following morning. I had completely missed the dark of night because of its brief appearance that time of year. As I peered out over the pristine terrain from the door of the tent, I felt completely engulfed in something far greater than myself. Words cannot adequately express the emotions that ran through my body and soul. Perhaps it was because I was alone in the wilderness with no outside pressures or distractions. I can only describe it as the overwhelming presence of the Lord in the beauty of His unspoiled creation.

As I searched for a way to explain my emotions, I discovered that David's words from the Psalms best describe what I experienced: "O Lord, you have searched me and you know me. You know when I sit and when I rise; you perceive my thoughts from afar. You discern my going out and my lying down; you are familiar with all my ways. Before a word is on my tongue you know it completely, O Lord. You hem me in—behind and before; you have laid your hand upon me. Such knowledge is too wonderful for me, too lofty for me to attain. Where can I go from your Spirit? Where can I flee from your presence? If I go up to the heavens, you are there; if I make my bed in the depths, you are there. If I rise on the wings of the dawn, if I settle on the far side of the sea, even there your hand will guide me, your right hand will hold me fast. If I say, 'Surely the darkness will hide me and the light become night around me,' even the darkness will not be dark to you; the night will shine like the day, for darkness is as light to you" (Psalm 139:1-12).

After several moments of contemplation, I was interrupted by the aroma of hot coffee floating up the hill from the cook tent. Overwhelmed by the smell of frying bacon, I descended to the cook tent to begin another day in the great outdoors. After a great breakfast, we packed our lunches, grabbed our gear, and  trekked down the slippery hillside for a full day of fishing.

We were blessed to have Russ and Rich, two tireless and talented young guides who shared their time between our group and the others. They were willing to venture wherever we wanted to go and were always nearby for both protection and assistance, which by the way, I needed on more than one occasion. Several times I found the fly hook deeply imbedded into my neck, backside, or vest while trying to hurl it out in the gusting wind. I'm sure they enjoyed a few laughs at the end of the day at this rookie's expense. There were also a few occasions when a big grizzly decided not to spook, despite our waving and yelling. A little more warning encouragement from their shotguns always did the trick.

Our group hiked four miles north of camp, about halfway to the base of the volcano. We fished the river all the way up the bay and then followed another stream back southward toward the ocean. We ended up on the opposite side of the bay from camp. Everyone had caught a lot of nice fish by noon. The numbers varied depending on who was telling the story.

We had romped through the heart of bear country all the way and never had an encounter. There were many tracks on the east side of camp but we saw no bears. Later, we climbed up a giant sand dune for a better vantage point to relax and have lunch. Camp was visible about a mile or so across the bay. The Pacific was directly over the dune behind us and to our right was a large meadow with lush, deep grass. As we enjoyed our sandwiches, we noticed a large tan bear and two cubs beginning to move through the meadow in our direction a few hundred yards away. We had been warned about the dangers of a female with cubs. Their maternal instinct to protect their offspring could cause them to attack if they sensed danger. As the bears got closer, we found ourselves sitting up and paying more attention. It was a good opportunity for photographs. We might not get that close again all week, so I shot away. Little did I know what was to come tomorrow. Within a few minutes, the bears were about 100 yards away. This was as close as we had been to bears since we arrived. We were downwind and she did not see or smell us until she got to the river just below the dune where we were perched. Russ thought that was too close for comfort so we all stood up together, waving and yelling. She stood up on her hind legs and pawed the air in our direction, the cubs hiding behind her in the grass. She soon turned and moved away, heading up river for a more peaceful place to fish. That was easy!

After lunch we walked down the Pacific side of the dune to see if fish were biting in the ocean breakers. We waded out about 50 yards before the water got too deep. The wind was blowing hard and waves would hit with ice-cold spray. Some seals were swimming a few yards in front of us, probably gathering fish for lunch. They were difficult to keep in sight because of the breaking waves and the wind-blown spray. From time to time one would raise its head out of the water and I could see its big eyes looking curiously in our direction. Then like lightning, one swam in front of me at blazing speed and charged Rusty, nipping at his leg as it passed by. We took that as a sign we were trespassing and headed for dry land.

We proceeded along the shoreline to the mouth of the bay, directly across from the steep hill where our camp was located several hundred yards inland. The banks of the hill were very steep with long claw-like fingers of volcanic rock extending out into the ocean. They curved on around the coastline as far as we could see. As we investigated these odd outcroppings we found other volcanic rocks had fallen from the rocky cliffs above and were lodged between the crevasses amongst a myriad of clam and mussel shells. There were millions of them stacked on top of and beside each other as far as the eye could see.

What I found especially interesting was the shape of the rocks. They must have been there for centuries. The rocks on the cliffs were mostly square and rectangular chunks of volcanic stone but these rocks of various sizes were almost all perfectly round. When a wave

rolled in and covered the spires, all the rocks trapped in the crevasses were likewise rolled backward, then tumbled forward as the water receded. Years, even centuries of being washed in the waves of the ocean had smoothed the once rough and brittle edges into perfect circles. I was reminded of God's principle of how the washing of His Word produces perfection in our lives and smoothes our rough edges.

That evening after dinner, standing on the side of the cliff and looking down toward the outcroppings we had explored earlier, I spotted a male moose on the beach with his mate. They were contently grazing on some vitamin-enriched kelp that had washed ashore. The moose weren't nearly as impressed with the rocks as I was. In fact, the rocks made their navigation of the coastline much more difficult and were simply a nuisance to them. But what did they care? After all, they had each other, a beautiful place to live, and a protein-rich dinner to satisfy their needs. They couldn't have been more content. It was just the close of another routine day in the great outdoors.

My heart, the sun hath set.
Night's paths with dews are wet.
Sleep comes without regret;
Stars rise when sun is set.
All's well. God loves thee yet,
Heart, smile, sleep sweet, not fret.

WILLIAM QUAYLE

TOO CLOSE FOR COMFORT

ON A BRIGHT, SUNNY MORNING, Rusty, our guide Rich, and I hiked to the upper river near a mountain called Homer Hill, just south of the volcano. Fishing along the way, we caught pinks and chums with almost every cast. Suddenly Rusty spotted a large eagle's nest in a tree beside the rocky cliff above and stopped just beneath it for photographs. The female was perched on a limb above the nest basking in the warm sun as the heads of the young eaglets peered out from their lofty home.

We proceeded down the river, stopping on a gravel bed in a narrow fork to fish both sides. Always cognizant of our proximity to bears, I observed what I thought was a bear about 300 yards west of us. We were deep in bear territory—alder trees were very thick on the hillside above the bank. I yelled "bear" to warn the others. We were accustomed to seeing several bears by now, but were still very cautious, making a lot of noise as we walked. What I thought was a bear turned out to be a large caribou grazing behind some alder trees beside the river. I didn't see its head behind the brush. When he began moving in our direction, we sat down in the gravel and became very still. He walked up within 20 yards of where we were seated. He was a magnificent creature—a large buck with a huge rack, just beginning to shed the velvet from his towering horns. He was as curious as we were and pranced around for several minutes, grazing in the lush grass along the shore and casually observing us as he looked up between bites. We took this opportunity to take several photos. As we slowly stood up, he turned and trotted a few steps away, moving closer to the brushy hillside but still pretty close.

It was beginning to mist so we put our cameras safely away in our backpacks and resumed our quest of salmon, keeping an eye on the caribou from time to time. The peaceful sounds of the rippling river were suddenly interrupted by the loud shatter of cracking tree limbs. The caribou flinched and jerked his head up from the grass, looking into the brush on the hillside. In a fraction of a second, a huge grizzly leaped from the thicket in an attempt to catch the caribou. His eyes were fixed like radars on the big buck. Hungry and meaning business, he let out a vicious growl, exposing his huge teeth. The three of us froze like stones on that gravel bed. All we could move was our eyes as we watched the ensuing chase.

The massive bear pounded the water as he pursued the caribou across several divisions in the river, snarling loudly all the way. The caribou had a decisive lead and escaped in the flat just south of the volcano where he had been grazing moments before. I could not believe my eyes. None of us could. It was by far the largest bear we had seen all week and certainly the closest we had been to one. Not one of us got a picture of the event. Quite honestly, it never entered our minds until the entire incident was over. We had missed the photograph of a lifetime but thankfully escaped with a memory we will never forget. When both animals were out of sight, we sat down on

the gravel bar in dead silence. There were no words to describe what had just happened.

When we could finally feel our hearts beating again, we went back to fishing. I looked up to watch the male eagle on his approach back to his family in the nest. He was a magnificent specimen with a wingspan of about seven or eight feet. He circled three times about 50 feet above and dove close enough for photos. My camera was back around my neck. I had learned my lesson— rain or not—it was not going back in the pack.

Once again we spotted the frustrated bear along the river in the same spot where I had first seen the caribou. Assuming our frozen positions, we made certain this time to have our cameras ready. He continued following the river directly toward us. He was now about 100 yards away and Rich wasted no time getting his shotgun in the ready position. All we could do was stand there and hope he would turn away. But he kept coming and was now on the bank of the river about 30 yards away. We jumped up, waving and yelling, but he didn't turn away. He was mad. He had lost the caribou and was hungry and very frustrated. As we continued to wave and yell, he stood up on his hind legs and shook his head from side to side growling and pawing. I managed to snap some great photographs of the massive carnivore as he continued his angry display for several moments before finally turning and lumbering off in search of salmon. When he disappeared out of sight, we decided that was enough action for one day and made the long hike back to camp to share our amazing story with our comrades. This was one fishing story they surely could not top!

That evening after dinner we sat on the windy cliff above the bay and watched several bears as they fished for salmon. It is an incredible sight to see these huge clumsy-looking creatures calmly stalk a fish from the shore, charge the icy water, and in the blink of an eye, retrieve it. Salmon provide most of the diet necessary for hibernation. This time of year, bears consume 80 to 90 pounds of food daily in order to gain 3 or 4 pounds of fat. During the summer salmon runs, they will gain several hundred pounds to sustain them through months of hibernation. As I pondered this fact, I thought how the three of us on the gravel bar would

have been enough food to last the bear almost a week.

Another exciting adventure drew to a close as the sunlight began to cast long shadows across the bay. After all the bear and fish stories of the day had been shared, one of the older gentlemen in camp stood up and commented while staring across the expansive panorama, "How insignificant we humans are when compared to the vastness of earth."

It is easy to feel insignificant in comparison to this overwhelming landscape of 8,000-foot mountains and giant grizzlies. Though dwarfed by the magnitude of the land and amazed by the potentially dangerous wildlife, I was comfortable and at peace in the wilderness even though I think I still slept with one eye open.

The sportsman lives his life vicariously—for he secretly yearns to have lived before, in a simpler time. A time when his love for the land, water, fish and wildlife would be more than just part of his life—it would be his state of mind.

JIM SLINSKY

THE
RIDE OF A
LIFETIME

EQUALLY EXCITING as the bear and caribou encounter was the helicopter ride to an adjacent bay the following day. The experience was exhilarating. The sights were incredible as we flew from the bay over the mountains, exploring areas that were unreachable by any other means of transportation.

Our early morning flight took us over the snowcapped cauldron of an ancient volcano. A herd of caribou was pawing through the thin layer of snow, nipping at the tender new shoots of grass. As we glided and turned, soaring at great speeds on the powerful wind currents of the Pacific, we were able to see for miles in all directions.

After crossing the mountain, we swooped down into a lush valley where several bears were grazing with their cubs. Many stood up in amazement, standing on their hind legs and pawing as though they wanted to knock us out of the sky. We observed a number of eagles that were similarly startled from the roar of the helicopter and rose from their nests in flight.

We ascended another mountain and caught our first glimpse of the next bay. A dense fog covered everything and for a moment, we were engulfed as well. As we descended to 50 feet above the surface, we regained visibility and the pilot set the chopper down on the beach. Four of us got off and quickly gathered our gear for a day of fishing. As soon as we were clear, he signaled and took off. He would return for us in six hours.

It was dark and dreary with a heavy mist in the air from the dense fog. The shoreline was completely covered with bear tracks of all sizes. The bay was narrow and several rivers fed into it from the

mountains just north of us. Large rock pinnacles blanketed in thick fog stood like sentinels jutting out into the barely visible Pacific Ocean.

Across a nearby meadow, I spotted a large female bear with two cubs walking away from us. Thankfully, the helicopter had spooked her into moving the opposite direction. Three of the guys decided to fish the river just beyond the shore where we had landed. I chose to video the area while it wasn't yet raining.

As I zoomed in on the top of the pinnacle, I discovered a large eagle's nest. A female sat on the rocks just above and I could distinguish the heads of several eaglets peering from their lofty home. After several minutes of walking with the viewfinder to my eye, I realized I was standing almost directly beneath the pinnacle. Just as I began to lower the camera, the female swooped down in my direction. I flinched and ducked as she flew past. I had infringed on her territory and she was not a happy mother.

Bald eagles have superb eyesight which enables them to spot a fish from high in the air and then dive on wingspans up to seven and eight feet at speeds approaching 100 miles per hour. Their powerful talons can strike with twice the force of a rifle bullet.

I quickly retreated and she returned to her perch just above the nest. I proceeded to walk along the shore, frequently looking back over my shoulder to make certain she remained on the rocks. Sitting at the very top of a nearby pinnacle disguised in the fog was a large male eagle, certain to be the mate of the one I had just encountered.

As I began to video him, the female rose from her perch and flew back to join him on top of the slender stone. The two beautiful birds sat breast to breast and looked at each other. After a few moments, they touched their beaks together in what appeared to be a kiss and the male immediately flew out over the ocean disappearing into the fog. The female had placed her order for lunch and he went out to pick it up!

I sat on the beach for 15 minutes and watched as she returned to her eaglets. After about a half hour, the male returned to the nest with a fish and everyone enjoyed a nice meal together. Both genders are notoriously good parents and often alternate sitting on the nest and caring for their young. I was so thankful for the up-close and personal observation.

While I had been eagle watching, the other guys were catching salmon with every cast. The fish were swimming into the bay by the thousands and making their way upstream to spawn. I joined in on the action for a couple of hours until my arms got so tired from catching fish that I decided to do some more exploring.

I persuaded our guide Russ to take me to a large waterfall a couple of miles up river so I could get some pictures. He was more than happy to accommodate me and the two of us set out along the river, stopping occasionally to observe large numbers of salmon. Some of the fish had arrived at their destination and were preparing their nests in the gravel near the bank of the river. The water was crystal clear. It was amazing to watch them dig a hole with their tails and arrange the rocks with their snouts. Some nests already contained pink eggs and the salmon hovered over them for protection.

We continued our quest, making a lot of noise to spook away any bears lurking behind the thick brush. As we grew closer to the waterfall, the river current grew much stronger. The determined salmon, anxious to make it to their destination, fought tirelessly against the force of the water.

We turned at a bend in the river and from behind the brush we saw the raging water. It was so loud we could barely hear each other. As we got closer, no bears were awaiting us but salmon were jumping from the river trying to reach the top of the waterfall. The homing instinct and the determination of the salmon is truly one of life's great miracles. It was a stunning sight as the icy water poured through a narrow fog-filled canyon falling several feet below into a crystal clear pool filled with fish.

We sat down on a gravel bed and removed some of our gear to lighten the load. I proceeded to photograph while Russ climbed a steep rock cliff to reach the top of the waterfall. I would have joined him if nothing else to prove that a 50-year-old guy could keep up with a 20-something, strapping young man, but unfortunately we were on a tight schedule and couldn't afford to miss our afternoon flight out.

We joined the other fishermen at the coast a few minutes before our chopper arrived. By now the fog was too heavy to fly back over the hills so we proceeded to fly along the coastline just above the water until we reached our bay. When we turned the corner leading into our bay, the sun was shining and it was a clear, beautiful view. No fog! My senses were completely overloaded with the drastic weather changes, the dramatic views from the helicopter, and studious observations of the eagles, bears, and fish.

I will lie down and sleep in peace, for you alone, O LORD, make me dwell in safety.

THE BOOK OF PSALMS

THE CYCLE OF LIFE

THE MOST FASCINATING TRUTH I learned from my week in the wilderness was taught by the salmon. Swimming with all their might, jumping head first into roaring waterfalls, and fighting swift currents, they seek the exact location of their birth to give life to a new generation. They are a perfect example of fulfilling their calling.

The life cycle of the Pacific salmon begins after the male and female make a perilous journey upstream from the sea and undergo a physical transformation that prepares them for reproduction known as spawning. Salmon are anadromous fish, meaning they hatch in fresh water, migrate out to salt water in the sea, and then return to the fresh water where they originated to spawn. Some varieties stay in fresh water from one to three years while most stay only a few months.

Salmon spend up to seven years in the food-rich ocean growing rapidly from its nutrients. They have a strong homing instinct that drives them back to their fresh water birth stream to spawn. It is fascinating how each succeeding generation of the salmon population will return to the same spawning grounds as prior generations. They locate their birth streams through their sense of smell. It is mind-boggling that they can leave a remote fresh water stream, swim into the vastness of the Pacific Ocean, and return years later to the exact spot of their birth.

As the predominantly silver-colored salmon enter the stream, a transformation takes place and the silver changes to vibrant hues of reds, purples, and greens. These bright colors allow the different species to identify their mates at spawning time. During this transformation in the fresh water, the adult fish do not feed and their physical condition begins to deteriorate.

Seas roll to waft me, suns to light me rise;
My footstool earth, my canopy the skies.

ALEXANDER POPE

Once the female salmon reaches her exact spawning ground, she digs a nest with her tail and snout in the gravel of the stream to lay her eggs. This activity attracts the males who defend their breeding rights by swimming into and biting each other. The male swims alongside the female and fertilizes her eggs as soon as they are laid. The female may release several batches of eggs over a period of a few days. After they are fertilized, she covers them with gravel for protection and defends them for about a week until her death.

In a few days, the tiny inch-long salmon emerge from their eggs. They receive life-sustaining nourishment and oxygen from a tiny yolk sac that is attached to their abdomen. Once they lose their yolk sacs and mature into fingerlings, their color changes and they blend into the gravel, thus camouflaging them from predators. They are now large enough to rely on small aquatic insects for food.

Some varieties remain in the fresh water for a year or more while others move almost immediately to salt water of the Pacific. Before migration down stream to the ocean, the young salmon go through a process called smoltification, which completes their transition from fresh water to salt water.

During their life in the ocean, some varieties may travel thousands of miles. They feed off plankton, crustaceans, and other small fish, and grow rapidly before returning to their ancestral spawning grounds. After spawning, the adult salmon die. Their decomposing bodies provide food for bears, birds, and predators and rich nutrients for the soil. Their newly fertilized eggs become the next generation of salmon that will repeat the same life cycle of those who have gone before them.

An interesting analogy can be drawn from the life cycle of the salmon. First of all, they function exactly like God designed them. After their miraculous birth, they remain close to their nest feeding from a yolk sac, much the same way humans receive all of the necessary life-giving nutrients from mother's milk. New Christians receive the milk of God's Word, learning the simple truths of the Gospel from "fishers of men."

As they mature in size, the young salmon venture out of their nest exploring new territory, learning to swim and feed themselves. Humans follow much the same order. Infants move from crawling to walking and graduate from milk to feeding themselves softer foods and meat. As young Christians mature, they move from the milk of God's Word to exploring the real meat—learning to read, study, and apply biblical principles on their own.

When the salmon are mature enough, they swim out into the vast ocean to grow and enjoy the freedom and fullness of life the sea has to offer. When humans are physically mature enough, they leave the security of their families and venture out into the vast world to make a life of their own, discovering all the opportunities that await them. When the young Christian reaches maturity, he or she ventures out into this world enjoying the freedom of the Gospel, sharing the good news with others as "fishers of men."

God in His perfect love has chosen to share His creation and its wonderful cycle of life with each of us. We can definitely learn a lesson from the salmon. Live life to the fullest—never take it for granted. It is a gift from above to be enjoyed, nurtured, conserved, and shared. Never view yourself as an insignificant part of God's grand creation. It is, after all, the determined salmon and the mighty bear that are satisfied to live and die in the wilderness, fulfilling their purpose on earth, never to live again. We humans have the wonderful option of spending eternity with our heavenly Father.

While we are often overwhelmed by the magnificence and beauty of creation all around us, it is important to remember that He loved man more than any other part of His creation and sent His son to walk among us beside the sea, sharing stories with His fishing buddies about a place called Heaven; a place more beautiful than anything mankind has ever seen before; a place far greater than anything we have experienced in the great outdoors. We are indeed wonderfully blessed.

The best remedy for those who are afraid, lonely, or unhappy
is to go outside, somewhere where they can be quiet, alone with the
heavens, nature, and God. Because only then does one feel
that all is as it should be and that God wishes to see people happy,
amidst the simple beauty of nature.

ANNE FRANK